MIND SHIFT

ADRIAN J.R. Davis

www.TrueVinePublishing.org

Mind Shift
Adrian J.R. Davis

Published by
True Vine Publishing Co.
810 Dominican Dr.
Nashville TN 37228
www.TrueVinePublishing.org

ISBN: 978-1-962783-00-2 Paperback
ISBN: 978-1-962783-01-9 eBook

Printed in the United States of America—First Printing

DEDICATION

This book is in remembrance and dedication to my oldest brother and first hero, Thomas Davis III. Thank you for all you gave me in life and all that you are giving me in your death. I appreciate you for energizing me to carry on my life's mission with more passion and determination, now, more than ever. Because of you, many will know that there is life beyond work and that we all should look to enjoy our lives while we are here on planet earth. Your memories will always stay with me and others who want to learn more about you.

TABLE OF CONTENTS

WELCOME TO THE SHIFT

Welcome to a journey of discovery and growth. In the pages ahead, it is my desire to create a shift in your thinking about life, success, and personal development. You see, I believe most people wander through this life as though looking through a mirror. Everything looks clear and as it should be, but in actuality, everything you are seeing is reversed. What is on your right, is actually your left.

I have learned through my career, failures and successes, that what I thought was right was wrong and that I needed to completely shift my thinking. In this book, I will uncover the true factors that may be keeping your from achieving your greater sense of self.

You will learn the powerful philosophy that will guarantee that you get help from people who can push you toward your goals–a principle we'll come to know as the 3X philosophy. This will be our guiding light through this voyage of self-improvement.

As we dive in, we'll unravel practical steps for asking for help in a smart way. You'll discover that seeking assistance isn't a sign of weakness, but rather a brave step toward becoming the best version of yourself. Remember, it's not just about receiving, but also about giving.

Throughout our journey, you'll find that success isn't just about luck or talent. It's about being ready for the

<7>

opportunities that come our way. We'll learn to under-stand ourselves better and set clear goals, essential tools in this adventure. Along the way, we'll encounter advice for success, but remember, it's your dreams and ambi-tions that will shape your unique path.

Each chapter will conclude with a recipe for success and change. As we stand on the threshold of this journey, armed with knowledge and courage, let's take the first step together. Let's be open to helping and being helped, to creating value, and to propelling ourselves towards a future filled with purpose and impact. The power is in our hands, and together, we have the ability to shape a world brimming with endless possibilities. Are you ready to embark on this journey? Let's begin.

<8>

THE POWER OF COMMUNITY

"Bro!"

That's how my conversations with my best friend and business partner Tim always kick off. We can gauge the vibe of our talk based on the energy and emphasis we put into that first word, Bro. If it's low, there's a problem. If it's energized, get ready for an amazing idea. This time, it was different. It was louder and more joyous than ever before.

"I've got this idea for a wealth-building partnership," he continued.

He had my attention. "Go on," I urged.

"Let's start putting money into a savings account to get ready for a big investment opportunity."

Tim had been devouring "The Richest Man in Babylon" and was fired up. Without a second thought, I replied, "Let's do it."

We drew up our plan, complete with rules, monthly meet-ups, assigned reading, and more. As time passed, we began to see our efforts pay off. Investments were yielding impressive returns. Yet, beyond the financial gains, we had created something even more valuable. We'd built a support network and nurtured a community of like-minded achievers. It was an unspoken pact to always be a source of guidance.

This community has been the wind beneath my wings in reaching my goals. When I felt like throwing in

<9>

the towel due to obstacles, they lifted me up with words of encouragement, inspiration, and even some tough love. They urged me to keep moving forward, even in the darkest moments. I'll repeat that: "keep moving forward in the darkness." Getting a second wind doesn't mean you suddenly have everything figured out or that you can see the light at the end of the tunnel. You might still be in the dark. The key is to keep going, trusting that sooner or later, the light will shine through. You'll still have doubts, fears, and moments of uncertainty about whether you're on the right path. But eventually, the light will come, and you'll find yourself at your destination.

I haven't reached my ultimate goal just yet, but I can echo the words of Martin Luther King, Jr.: I've been to the mountaintop. I'm at a place where I can see the way forward. It's like having a panoramic view of my destination. And honestly, I didn't get here by myself. It's because of my community—the people with whom I chose to share my dreams, ideas, and aspirations.

Much like a ship's crew is essential for its voyage, your community plays a crucial role in your journey towards success. While your personal goals and drive set the course, it's the collective force of your community that steers the ship.

Imagine a young explorer at a bustling career fair, faced with a world of potential professions. Among the options, the booth labeled "Astrophysicist" calls out, promising a journey into the cosmos and the mysteries of

<10>

the universe. This encounter ignites a spark within the dreamer, who envisions a future as an astrophysicist, an adventurer among the stars.

Excitedly, he shares his newfound passion with his peers, only to be met with skepticism and laughter. Their doubts become a tempest, challenging his newfound confidence. Even a well-meaning teacher suggests a more "practical" path. Undeterred, he returns home, eager to share his dream with his family, only to face further skepticism. Each encounter chips away at his resolve, burying the once-vibrant seed of ambition beneath layers of uncertainty.

This tale of the determined dreamer battling against a tide of doubt is a familiar one. Many seeds of potential find themselves stifled before they have a chance to grow. This is where the science of the environment comes into play. In sociology, a community is defined as a group adhering to a specific social structure within a larger society, encompassing elements like culture, norms, values, and status. Communities work together to organize social life in a particular location, and their cohesion may also be driven by a shared sense of identity that endures across time and space. This sense of belonging across temporal and spatial boundaries is a crucial aspect to emphasize in this definition.

It's fascinating to observe that the more time individuals spend with a particular group or person, the more likely they are to internalize certain traits and behaviors.

<11>

This phenomenon essentially implies that spending time together leads to behavioral alignment.

Culture is a rich reservoir of knowledge, experiences, beliefs, values, attitudes, meanings, hierarchies, religious practices, notions of time, roles, spatial relationships, conceptualizations of the universe, and material possessions that a community accumulates over generations through both individual and collective efforts. The noteworthy element in this definition is the reference to the transmission of culture "through the course of generations."

This brings to mind an anecdote by Zig Ziglar: A young newly-married woman was preparing her first Christmas ham for the holiday dinner. Her new husband looked on with confusion as she pulled out a knife and began cutting the ends of the ham off.

"What are you doing?" he questioned.

"I'm cutting off the ends of the ham."

"I see that, but why?" he inquired.

"I don't know. That's the way my mom did it."

Amused, the husband continued his investigation. "I've got to hear this. Let's call your mom and find out why she would do that."

The couple called the wife's mom and asked.

"Mom, why did you cut the ends off of the ham?" she asked.

"I did it because that's how my mom cooked the ham," she responded.

<12>

So the group called the wife's grandmother and asked, "Grandmom, why did you cut the ends of the ham off of the Christmas ham?"

The grandmother said, "I cut the ends of the ham off because my pot was too small."

The story reveals how behaviors can be passed down without questioning, even when the original reasons no longer apply. Our daily actions and perspectives can be heavily influenced by communal norms. We might benefit from considering whether these perspectives remain ideal for our personal circumstances.

Norms, integral to the social sciences, are rules or expectations that receive social enforcement. They can be prescriptive, encouraging positive conduct (e.g., "be honest"), or proscriptive, discouraging negative behavior (e.g., "do not cheat").

Values, on the other hand, represent ideals or principles that determine what is morally right, desirable, or correct. These intangible beliefs are embraced and upheld by a given society. In simpler terms, values guide individuals in recognizing what is worthy and worth striving for. As Haralambos aptly defines, a value is a belief that encapsulates something as good and worthwhile.

Status pertains to an individual's position in a group or society, often in relation to others. It is marked by specific benefits and responsibilities, shaped by an individual's rank and role within the social structure.

<13>

The field of environmental sociology delves into the intricate dynamics of communities, their shared norms, values, and behaviors, and how these elements traverse generations. It's a reminder that our perceptions are often shaped by the contexts we're exposed to, and a call to critically evaluate whether these inherited viewpoints align with our own needs and circumstances.

Definition of Achieved Status

(noun) A status that is acquired or earned as the result of personal accomplishment and merit, that serves as a reflection of ability, choice, or personal effort.

Definition of Ascribed Status

(noun) A status assigned at birth or assumed involuntarily later in life, often based on biological factors, that cannot be changed through individual effort or achievement.

Definition of Master Status

(noun) The primary identifying status of an individual that shapes interactions and relationships with others and dominates all other statuses.

Birds of a Feather Flock Together

Homophily, the natural tendency to gravitate towards those who share our interests and characteristics, is a social phenomenon that holds significant sway. In simpler terms, it's our inclination to be drawn to people who are similar to us.

This concept forms the basis of the age-old saying,

<14>

"Birds of a feather flock together." This ancient adage simply suggests that individuals with common interests and backgrounds tend to find kinship with one another. It's a notion that transcends cultural boundaries and persists through generations.

Consider the familiar scenarios of school days, like wondering, "Is this where the cool kids sit?" or hoping to gain entry into an exclusive social circle. As adults, we might not voice it as plainly, but the sentiment remains: "I'd like to join your group because I believe we share similar values and interests."

We've all experienced the longing for a sense of belonging, whether in the early school years or later stages of education. From preschool to college, those moments of camaraderie leave indelible marks on our memories. This sense of unity doesn't fade with age.

One poignant memory comes to mind: my daughter, still in preschool, once mused while sitting in her back of the car, "I think Sara is really pretty. I want her to be my best friend." Of course, my first job was to affirm and reassure her of her own beauty. Afterward, I delved deeper. It turns out, it wasn't just about appearances. Sara was, by unanimous consent, the most popular kid in the school. The desire for friendship was intertwined with the allure of being associated with Sara.

Who among us hasn't contemplated joining a club, fraternity, or group for the social credibility it will bring us? It's a universal inclination. Yet, there's a deeper com-

<15>

plexity to this pursuit of belonging. When we reflect on who we aspire to be, it's not merely a matter of popularity. We seek to make a meaningful impact, to lead a purpose-driven life. However, stepping into that role may require reevaluating our social circles, potentially reshaping our core identities. This crossroads is where many find themselves.

Regrettably, without a clear plan, countless individuals grapple with this internal conflict, leading to lives marked by internal dissonance. If you resonate with this struggle and are eager for change, read on. We'll explore strategies to help pave the way towards your envisioned life.

Social Psychology Phenomenon of mirroring
The Outcome Pyramid Demystified:

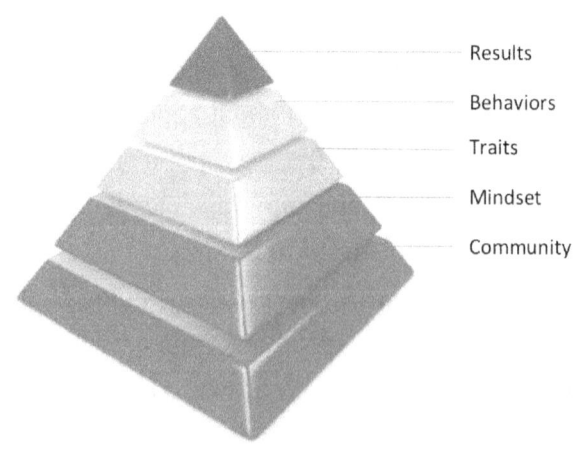

Results

Behaviors

Traits

Mindset

Community

<16>

At the foundation of our personal growth lies an invisible force I call the Outcome Pyramid. It's a structure with five crucial levels: Community, Mindsets, Traits, Behaviors, and Results. Often, we look at our outcomes, wondering why our lives turn out the way they do. I propose a fresh perspective.

The sequence of these levels matters immensely. Tackling them in order ensures that you're investing your time and effort in the right areas for the outcomes you desire.

"Imagine two colleagues in the same organization, doing the same work, both earning the same amount of money. Yet, one of them is thriving, happy, and successful, while the other is weighed down by debt and struggling to find contentment. It's a stark contrast, isn't it? But how can this be? That's what we're about to explore."

Let's kick off with what I believe is the most critical level: "Community." As we've discovered, a significant portion of our success or setback is influenced by this level. We might resist it, but certain things are just ingrained in us. It's how we're wired.

Community wields tremendous influence over the kind of life you lead. It plants the seeds for growth, nurtures them, and eradicates anything that threatens them. Its impact is subtle yet constant. Community shapes your language, physique, finances, outlook on life, and much more.

<17>

This is why achieving a goal can be incredibly tough if "the community" views it as foreign or undesirable. For instance, let's say you want to get in shape and cut out certain foods. If your community doesn't support this, you'll face questions like "Why?" They're not trying to sabotage your goal; they just can't fathom why you'd set such a goal in the first place. They genuinely believe they're looking out for your best interests.

These well-meaning folks will keep offering you those foods you're trying to avoid. They might even try to dissuade you from working out, asking you to just "chill" or "take it easy." Questions like "What's gotten into you?" become commonplace. For many, this is enough to deter them from pursuing their goal.

Let me be clear: the "community" is persistent and unyielding. It's part of their identity. The only way to change is to find a different community.

The second level of the pyramid is "mindset." As the late, great Bob Proctor put it, "We should hyphenate the word Mind-Set. It's a mind that is set in its ways." Your mindset is heavily influenced by the previous level, "community." Once the community has had its say, you're left with your mindset, your mental filter for interpreting the world.

It's a challenge to change someone's fixed mindset. They've been so shaped by their community that even when they're outside it, the community is still within them. Their beliefs and thought patterns are so deeply

<18>

ingrained that they struggle to see any other perspective. It's like speaking a different language.

Have you ever found yourself in a situation where no matter how many facts or logical explanations you presented, changing someone's mind seemed nearly impossible? Stuart Chase, a renowned author, economist, and engineer, encapsulated this phenomenon with his statement: "For those who believe, no proof is necessary. For those who don't believe, no proof is possible."

Your mindset wields tremendous power in how you interpret situations. If your perspective is inclined towards the negative aspects of a situation, positivity might struggle to find a foothold. Conversely, if you adopt a positive mindset, you're likely to perceive positivity even in challenging circumstances. You might be wondering, "Didn't we touch on something similar regarding the community?" Indeed, but this time, it's about your internal community—the beliefs and thought patterns you've absorbed. These thoughts become your own, shaping how you approach risk, navigate relationships, manage finances, and more.

This is precisely why two individuals facing similar circumstances can lead vastly different lives. Some may find themselves feeling like "victims" in their own narrative, while others rise to become "heroes" of their story.

Consider the profound impact of repetition on our beliefs. When something is reiterated consistently, it can feel like our own original idea. After a lifetime of expo-

<19>

sure to various ideas and influences, distinguishing between our independent thoughts and implanted ones becomes a challenge. Trust me, much of what we believe has been subtly ingrained.

Now, let's shift our focus from the internal, metaphysical aspects of the Outcome Pyramid to what the world perceives—the third level, "traits." Traits encompass the visible characteristics and behaviors that define an individual. They're the markers that prompt people to say, "That's just how they are."

These traits help us recognize if someone is acting out of character. You might hear comments like, "They didn't seem like themselves today." Essentially, what's being conveyed is that this person, who typically displays a specific set of traits, exhibited a different set on that particular day.

Traits essentially serve as labels for a set of behaviors. They offer insight into who a person is. While this understanding is crucial for those within our immediate circles, most of us don't consciously perceive the world in these terms. Instead, we intuitively decide whether we want to connect with a person or simply tolerate them until we can return to our familiar community.

<20>

Recipe for more/better results:

In this conversation, I've used health as an example to make a point, but it's worth noting that this approach can be applied to any area you want to improve. I often refer to this method as "Living an F'd Up Life," which means finding balance in five important areas: Family, Faith, Fun, Finance, and Fitness. I believe most people aim for some level of improvement in these aspects. Regardless of your focus, remember that concentrating on the process, not just the end results, is the key to making progress in the right direction.

Understanding the Underlying Causes:

Let's say you want to be a better parent and create a healthier family environment. Instead of just looking at your current situation, take a closer look at the behaviors you exhibit and try to understand why you act that way. This approach allows you to uncover the root causes of your experiences.

For instance, you might realize that your upbringing was in a community where parenting was mainly authoritarian, characterized by a "do as I say" approach. This was the norm not only in your home but also among your

<21>

friends' families and some of your extended relatives. Consequently, this is the model you grew up with, and it's influencing your parenting style today. However, if your co-parent comes from a completely different background, this approach may no longer align with your household's needs and your children's well-being.

Embracing a Shift in Mindset:

I want to clarify that I'm not prescribing a specific parenting style. What I'm suggesting is that you use this model to uncover the reasoning behind your results, which stem from your behaviors and traits. What you do with this insight is entirely up to you. If you aim to foster a family environment with different values, consider seeking out parents from diverse communities who embody those attributes. Engaging with them may take time, but it's a worthwhile investment.

Application in Various Areas:

This approach is universally applicable. Evaluate your outcomes, break down the behaviors and traits that contributed to them, and try to align a mindset with them. If successful, consider which community embodies this mindset and think about joining it to gain a fresh perspective. This, in turn, will lead to new behaviors and produce distinct results.

<22>

Navigating Community Differences:

I understand there might be reservations about immersing yourself in unfamiliar communities, and that's completely normal. You might initially find yourself saying, "I don't resonate with the way they communicate, behave, or present themselves in that community." This reaction is expected because your native community operates differently.

During my time working for the State of Tennessee, I held myself in high regard. I believed I set the standard just by walking into a room. However, upon closer examination, I realized I wasn't at the top of the hierarchy. Being who I am, I took the initiative to observe those who were. It became clear that they exhibited subtle differences in their conduct, communication, and work approach. It wasn't just their communication style; it extended to their financial management, social circles, and affiliations. I saw that there was more to it than just "putting pants on one leg at a time, just like I do." They operated differently.

Sometimes I found their conversations irritating, and the sentiment was mutual. The discomfort arose from a disparity in social norms. This is where labels like "snob" or "stuck up" come into play from one perspective, while others might perceive individuals as "not smart," "lazy," or "odd."

Contrary to the norms in my community, I took a step I hadn't been accustomed to—I reached out to some-

<23>

one from the different community for a conversation. This marked the inception of my journey to comprehend diverse thought patterns and perspectives (many of which hadn't even crossed my mind). I listened attentively to discover common ground and disparities. To my surprise, those whom I initially labeled as aloof turned out to be warm, down-to-earth individuals who simply viewed the world through a distinct lens.

I went on to ask some of them to be my mentors. What I gleaned from them, along with my own experiences, is what I'm eager to share in the rest of this book. Let's delve further.

<24>

THE GENESIS OF THE 3X PHILOSOPHY:

A Blueprint for Mutual Success

Around ten years ago, I discovered something important. As I started getting to know important people in
the business world, I noticed a pattern. While I was
building connections with these influential folks, I made
a point to offer some help, trying to show them that I
could be valuable. It was interesting to see that after
about three times of helping out, a chance would come
up for me to ask for their support. This is how I came up
with the 3X philosophy.

The 3X philosophy is pretty straightforward but
powerful: to do well in life, you have to be open to both
giving and getting help. It's based on the idea that when
you actively offer assistance to others at least three times,
it starts a natural cycle of support. This is the real heart
of the 3X philosophy: a deep understanding of the lasting
impact made through real connections, and the potential
for change that comes with them.

At its core, the 3X philosophy is all about give and
take. It recognizes that success doesn't usually happen
alone; it does best in a place of working together and
shared goals. It's not just about trading favors; it's a lively
back-and-forth that builds true friendships, tying people

<25>

together in the shared journey towards success. The 3X philosophy knows that every act of giving starts a chain reaction. It spreads through our social circles, matching with the basic human wish to be kind in return. This way, we plant seeds of kindness and grow a community that not only helps us in our journey but also boosts the dreams of those around us.

"Give before you get" is the core belief behind the 3X philosophy. It means that real success isn't just about what you gain, but about sharing value. This idea celebrates being selfless. By actively offering help and making others' lives better, you build trust and goodwill. This shows that you're committed to the happiness and success of those around you.

Giving before you get creates an atmosphere of plenty. When you freely share your skills, time, or resources, you make a space where being generous and kind is encouraged. This, in turn, encourages others to do the same, creating a culture of mutual help and shared success. This idea also knows that real relationships are built on give and take. By offering help without expecting something back right away, you create opportunities that happen naturally. It's not a strategy you plan out, but a real result of truly wanting to make a positive impact on others' journeys.

The 3X philosophy, which starts with "give before you get," reminds us that success isn't a solo journey. It grows in a group of people who lift each other up.

<26>

Through this way of doing things, you don't just make a group of trusted friends, but also open doors to new chances and ways for personal and group growth. Most importantly, it's a reminder that being generous isn't a one-time thing, but a continuous investment in the important relationships and shared successes in our lives.

The right time to ask

You don't have to try to be the smartest person around, and honestly, it's better not to aim for that. It's totally fine to admit it. Having trouble asking for help says more about you than the people you're asking. Lots of folks think they're being a bother when they ask for help. But that's not really true. What matters is how you ask, why you're asking, and how clear you are about it. Let's break down these parts one by one before we talk about changing your thinking on this.

The Ask:

The request for assistance, guidance, or direction should pertain to something you genuinely believe is beyond your current capability to attain independently. It's crucial to grasp this concept because it complements your intentions and brings clarity to your goals.

When you acknowledge the need for help and are open to seeking it, be proactive in researching who can offer you the most effective, efficient, and prompt assistance. If this person is not already in your network, take

<27>

the time to familiarize yourself with them. Understand their strengths and why it aligns with your request for help.

If, like me, you were raised with the mindset of striving to be the most knowledgeable and capable person in the room, consider that there's another perspective. While diligence and excellence are valuable attributes, they may not always lead you to reach out to subject matter experts for their guidance. This approach might suggest that you master every aspect of what you're seeking, which can be time-consuming. Instead, consider the wealth of knowledge likely available within close proximity.

I recall aspiring to become a national and international leadership trainer, and pondering the path to achieve that. I identified a prominent figure in the community and across the nation, someone who was well-known for their expertise in the industry. I took the initiative to connect with them. The initial challenge I faced was recognizing that I lacked a clear understanding of how to transition from my 9-5 role as an assistant to being sought after for speaking engagements nationwide.

The blueprint for this ambition appeared rather nebulous at first. However, the person I had in mind seemed to possess a clear sense of direction. So, I made the effort to locate them and humbly asked for their time and insights.

<28>

Here are three practical steps to seeking assistance effectively:

1. Assess Your Need for Help: Begin by evaluating whether the task or goal you're pursuing is something that genuinely exceeds your current capabilities. It's important to be honest with yourself about your limitations. This step ensures that you're seeking help for tasks that truly require it, rather than simply taking the easy way out. Understanding when to ask for assistance is a crucial first step..

2. Conduct Thorough Research: Once you've identified the need for help, take a proactive approach to find the most suitable person or resource. Research and identify individuals with the expertise and knowledge relevant to your specific request. This step is essential, especially if the right person isn't already within your existing network. Take the time to get to know them, understand their strengths, and determine how their expertise aligns with your needs.

3. Initiate Contact and Request Assistance: When you've identified the right person, reach out to them with a clear and concise request for assistance. Articulate your goals, challenges, and why you believe their expertise is valuable. It's crucial to be respectful of their time and to approach them with humility. Re-

<29>

member, seeking assistance is a sign of strength and a willingness to learn. Don't hesitate to ask for their insights, as their guidance can be invaluable in achieving your objectives.

Intention:

When asking for help, you must have the right intentions and you must be intentional.

Asking for help is a super important skill to have, but it's not just about saying, "Hey, can you help me?" It's also about having a clear reason why you need help. This is called having a pure intention. It means you're asking because you really need assistance, not just because it's easy or you don't want to figure things out on your own.

When you ask for help with pure intention, it shows that you respect the other person's time and knowledge. You're not wasting their time or taking advantage of them. You're saying, "I value you, your expertise, and I really need your guidance." This makes the person more likely to want to help you because they see that you're serious and genuinely need assistance.

Being intentional about asking for help also means thinking about who you're asking. You want to approach someone who has the knowledge or experience you need. It's like choosing the right tool for the job. When you're intentional, you're making a thoughtful decision about who can best assist you. This makes the whole process

<30>

more effective and helps you get the help you need faster.

You must also be intentional about your outcomes. When you approach someone for assistance, it's like setting out on a journey. You need to have a clear destination in mind. It means knowing exactly what you hope to achieve by seeking help. This clarity not only helps you express your needs better but also guides the person you're asking. They can offer more targeted advice or support when they understand your specific goals.

Additionally, being intentional about outcomes helps you take responsibility for the help you receive. It's like having a plan in place. You're not just hoping for the best; you're actively working towards a defined result. This mindset empowers you and makes you more proactive in utilizing the assistance you receive. You're not just leaving things up to chance, but rather, you're taking charge of your own success.

So, when you ask for help, have pure intentions for mutual benefit and growth. Put thought into who can best help you, and be intentional about what you truly want to achieve. This intentionality not only helps you communicate your needs effectively but also sets you on a clear path towards reaching your goals. It's a powerful way to make the most of the support you receive.

Here are three practical steps to effectively ask for help with intentionality and clear outcomes:

<31>

1. Define Your Objective: Before reaching out for assistance, take some time to clearly define what you want to achieve. Ask yourself: What specific outcome am I hoping for? What problem am I trying to solve? This step is crucial because it helps you communicate your needs more effectively. For example, if you're struggling with a math problem, be specific about which concept is causing confusion. This way, when you ask for help, you can provide clear information about what you're struggling with, making it easier for the person assisting you to provide targeted support.

2. Identify the Right Person: Consider who in your network or community has the expertise or experience to assist you with your specific goal. Look for individuals who have demonstrated knowledge in the area you need help with. This could be a teacher, a mentor, a colleague, or even a peer who excels in that subject or skill. Being intentional about who you approach ensures that you're seeking help from someone who is well-equipped to provide the guidance or information you need.

3. Express Your Needs Clearly and Concisely: When you approach someone for help, be direct and specific about what you're seeking. Clearly state your objective and the challenges you're facing. For instance, instead of saying, "I need help with this," you

<32>

could say, "I'm struggling with understanding the concept of fractions in math, and I'm looking for guidance on how to solve equations involving fractions." This way, the person you're asking for help understands exactly what you're looking for and can provide targeted support.

Clarity:

Finally, it's important to remember that a clear message makes it much easier for the person you're asking to give a helpful response. This is where many people stumble – they're not always clear in their requests. Some say it's easier to express what they don't want rather than what they do.

Have you ever been in a situation where someone asked you for something, and after their initial request, you were left with a bunch of questions? You might wonder what exactly they need, why they need it, how it should be done, and so on. In such cases, some folks might give up on the request altogether.

According to the DISC model, different people react differently in such situations. Some might seek more information to gain clarity, while others may think, "It's not my job to guess what they're thinking." Some might arrange a follow-up meeting, call, or email to get more details. It's crucial to realize that if a person is valuable or important to you, being unclear might make it harder for them to help you. They might think, "I shouldn't have to

<33>

work so hard to figure out what they really need from me."

I've personally experienced situations where someone told me to come back when I knew exactly what I wanted and could explain it clearly. It stung a little at the time, but looking back, it was incredibly helpful in the long run. It pushed me to be more precise and direct in my requests, which ultimately led to better outcomes.

Here are three ways to improve clarity when seeking assistance:

1. Be Specific and Concrete: Instead of using vague or general terms, provide clear and specific details. For example, rather than saying, "I need some help with this project," you could say, "I need assistance in analyzing the data for this project and creating a presentation summarizing the findings." This gives the person you're communicating with a clear understanding of what is expected.

2. Ask for Feedback: Seek input from others to ensure your message is coming across as intended. Ask questions like, "Can you please let me know if I've explained this clearly?" or "Is there anything that needs further clarification?" This allows you to address any potential misunderstandings early on and make necessary adjustments to improve clarity.

<34>

3. Use Visual Aids or Examples: Incorporate visual elements or provide examples to support your verbal or written communication. Charts, graphs, diagrams, and real-life examples can help illustrate your point and make complex information easier to grasp. For instance, if you're explaining a process, consider using a flowchart to visually represent the steps.

By implementing these strategies, you can significantly enhance the clarity of your communication, ensuring that your message is understood accurately by your audience.

Look for Ways to Add Value

Now that we've covered what makes a good request without bothering anyone, let's dive into the next step after identifying the person you want to ask. That step is simple: look for something you can do for them.

I can hear some reader murmuring now, "That seem manipulative. I don't want to do things just to get something in return." Well I have news for you, the entire universe works on this process. It's called cause and effect. We put a seed in the ground in order to get a fruit or a vegetable. We pay money to the movie theater to get entertainment in return. We offer time to a job to get money in return.

The Law of Reciprocity states that "when someone does something kind or helpful for us, we feel compelled to return the favor in kind." This is a universal law.

<35>

When you're seeking something you need, a great way to show your appreciation and seriousness is by finding a way to assist the person from whom you will request help. The difference of the 3X philosophy is that you offer this assistance, without expectation, first, not after they have helped you. Just remember, as long as your intentions are genuine and not misleading, you're on the right track.

I recall a time when I was introduced to a leadership coach by someone influential. I was truly impressed by how this coach managed his system and company. I wanted to get closer to him and understand more about his methods. That's when I put this 3X process into action.

I took a moment to figure out what mattered most to him and if there was a way I could contribute to those priorities. Even though I wasn't in a high-ranking position, I knew how to connect people and make persuasive cases.

The very next day, after meeting this coach and being inspired by his business expertise, I walked into my manager's office and declared, "We need this guy to speak at our conferences." My manager looked at me with a mix of surprise and concern. He responded, "Give me his information, and I'll review it." So, I provided all the necessary details and explained why this person would be a great fit for our audience.

While I was putting in this effort, my main goal was

<36>

to offer value to the coach I wanted to connect with. I also made sure he and his team knew I was the point person for any communication with my company regarding speaking or training opportunities.

Sure enough, his content and presentation on his website were so impressive that my company decided to bring him on for multiple projects. I made sure to stay visible throughout the process to show that he was partly there because of my introduction.

This is where transparency plays a key role. I wasn't doing this out of excessive kindness; I had a clear goal in mind. And it worked! After a few events where the coach was paid handsomely, he eventually reached out and said, "Would you like to be connected with me?" It started with free coaching opportunities and led to other ventures as well.

Give Before You Get

To truly get ahead, it's important to understand the concept of giving before receiving. If you're not sure how you can be of value to the person you're seeking help from, you're essentially leaving it up to chance for them to be generous or kind. While that's a noble idea, if you don't know the person well or understand their character, you're simply hoping for the best. When you become valuable, you put the onus on that person to make the right decision and encourage a sense of reciprocity.

<37>

Consider this: most actors spend more time honing their craft and trying to land their first significant role than they do actually being a top-tier actor. Similarly, many professional athletes dedicate years to building their skills before they can have a career that spans a fraction of their preparation time.

The same principle applies in other fields. The more effort you invest in improvement, the more opportunities you'll have to continue growing. However, in corporate settings, people often believe they have plenty of time to progress in their careers. This mindset can be limiting and deceptive. It's crucial to abandon this thought and realize that to achieve your goals, you must become proficient at something and be willing to give before you receive.

When you recognize that you've become skilled in a particular area, think about all the ways you can assist others. This becomes your gift, your product, or your contribution. It empowers you.

Reflect on my experience helping the leadership coach secure new business. I identified that I had the skill of networking and connecting people. I used this skill to get him something he truly wanted, making me valuable to him and his organization. As a result, I had the opportunity to get close to the coach, observe the inner workings of his company, and learn from his unique perspective on business and personal matters.

Lastly, let's discuss the optimal time to request help.

<38>

The timing depends more on your preparedness than on the person you're seeking assistance from. You need to be ready to offer three acts of service before receiving what you're seeking. Why three acts, you may wonder? It's about demonstrating your value and showing the person you're requesting help from that you're serious about helping them first.

In most cases, people are not unapproachable. They'll go out of their way to assist you once you've made your request. They may even try to outdo you in providing value. The return on your investment can be incredibly rewarding, often surpassing your initial efforts by a considerable margin.

My experience assisting the leadership coach brought me knowledge and access to a network I didn't know existed. Some of these connections have guided me through significant mental and logical shifts, leading to substantial financial gains since I first entered that community.

<39>

3X Recipe:

Here is the five-step process to help you obtain what you need and the support necessary for your journey towards success:

Step 1: Clearly understand your needs and don't hesitate to ask for assistance.

Step 2: Identify the right individual or group with the expertise to provide substantial help.

Step 3: Determine how you can offer assistance to them at least three times before seeking their help.

Step 4: Ask with confidence and clarity.

Step 5: Embrace and appreciate all the positive outcomes that come your way.

<40>

NAVIGATING YOUR JOURNEY:

Understanding Readiness for Success
Newness and Readiness Model

While you might believe you're fully prepared for your next major achievement, I'd like to offer a different perspective and a framework to help you navigate through moments of uncertainty.

Recognizing Your Readiness:

Being entirely prepared for every significant stride towards your life goals is an impossible feat. Think back to the last time you achieved something substantial - maybe it was landing a higher-paying job, moving into a new home, or getting a new car. In that moment of accomplishment, you weren't mentally geared up for what comes next. You were likely so immersed in the joy of your achievement that it consumed your thoughts for hours, days, or even weeks.

In faith-based communities, it's often said that you've just received a blessing. At that point, you're likely reveling in the blessing you've received, not yet contemplating the next one.

The truth is, there are approximately seven key emotional stages that you'll traverse before attaining your next significant reward, achievement, or blessing. Why is

<41>

this knowledge valuable? Because whether you're striving for something personally or leading a group, understanding these stages can help you gauge their readiness to embrace the next promotion, reward, new opportunity, or positive development.

Understanding Your Zones of Readiness

No matter who you are or where you stand in life, it's only natural to desire more, to seek improvement, and to aim for the next positive step in our journey. There's absolutely nothing wrong with this inclination. However, challenges arise when our aspirations seem to take longer to materialize than we expected. We're talking about life-altering events like finding a new home, meeting a life partner, switching jobs, or sealing a significant investment deal.

Reflecting on my own experience, I once owned a real estate investment for over a decade, hoping to take it to the next level. Initially, I didn't intend to be a landlord; my plan was to buy and renovate the property for a profitable resale, just as I had done numerous times before. But this time, it turned out differently.

As spring break approached, we were on the brink of closing the deal, anticipating a substantial payout. However, a neighborhood kid decided to use our freshly refurbished property as a canvas for their spray paint art. The unexpected call from my realtor informing me that the buyers wanted to back out was a shock. Suddenly,

<42>

$40,000 to $50,000 was hanging on this decision. I started asking questions: What happened? Who did this? Can it be fixed? Is there any way to salvage the deal? And so on.

Unfortunately, most of the answers led me to accept that the deal wasn't slipping away; it was gone. Due to the economic downturn in 2008, many potential buyers were holding onto their money, not making purchases. Now, I had to come to terms with the fact that I would be a landlord until the market improved.

Over the years, I had three major tenants, two of whom were good and one not so much. Through this experience, I gained invaluable insights into being a landlord. What I didn't grasp was how to expedite my exit from the landlord business. That's because I didn't know which zone of readiness I was in for my next significant move.

Before delving into these zones, it's important to note that some of them occur naturally over time. However, we do have the power to accelerate many of them if we understand our position and how to navigate the situation.

What research says:

Consider this: the average homeowner stays in their house for around 15 years. When it comes to cars, most people hold onto their vehicle for about eight years. Additionally, the typical employee stays in a job or position

<43>

for roughly four years. Why share these statistics? Well, it's because most individuals aspire to have a comfortable home, a reliable vehicle for transportation, and a job that not only pays the bills but also doesn't cause excessive stress. While there are other desires like finding a life partner, traveling to exotic destinations, or meeting a celebrity, the first set of goals is what the majority of people aim for.

Now, let's talk about how we can attain these things through deliberate intent and a structured approach in our lives. For instance, some may find it challenging to welcome a new life partner because they're entangled in conflicts with their current one. Similarly, some might struggle to step into a new job role because they're accustomed to dreading each day at work. The key takeaway here is that many of the things people say they want can be hindered by dwelling on how unsatisfactory their current or past situations were.

<44>

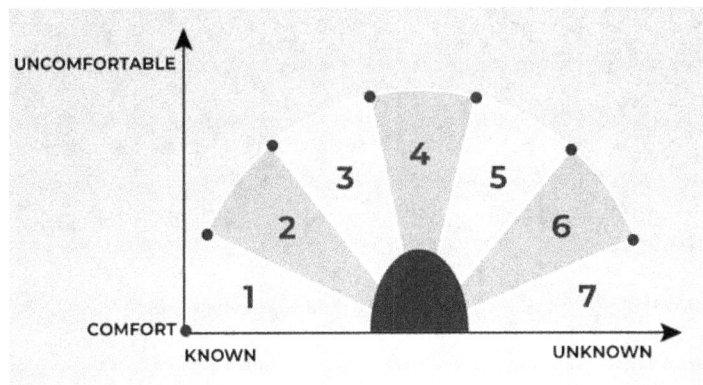

Figure 1.1

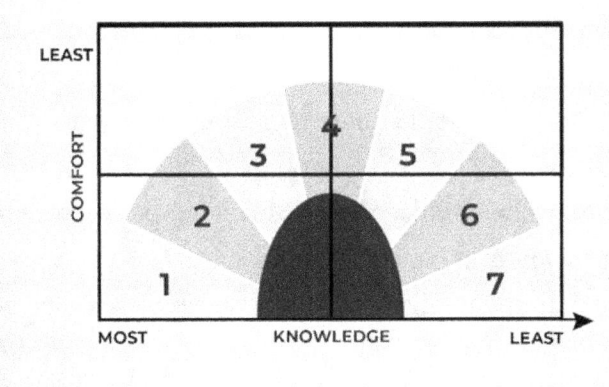

Figure 1.2

<45>

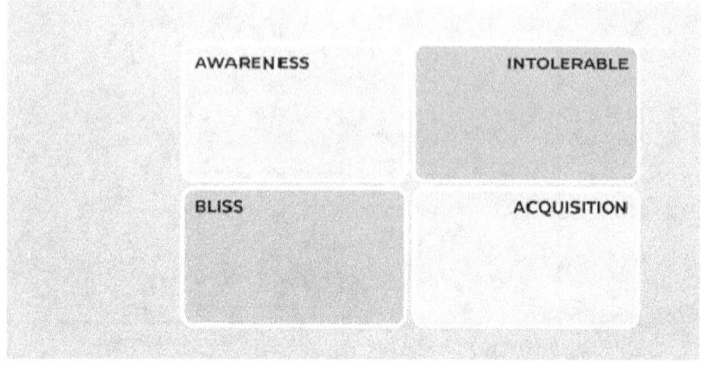

Figure 1.3

If you take a look at the image depicting Figures 2.1 and 2.2, you'll notice two axes: one representing comfort, and the other representing knowledge.

Comfort often holds many of us in places and situations that we should have moved on from years, or even decades, ago. It's been noted that change typically only occurs when the discomfort of staying put outweighs the fear of venturing into the unknown.

Within the figure, you'll see seven distinct zones. These zones symbolize the stages individuals commonly navigate when transitioning from familiarity to readiness for the next phase, which can be anything from a new job to a new mindset. Zones 1 through 3 fall within the "Bliss" quadrant, while zones 3 and part of 4 belong to the "Awareness" quadrant. Zones 4 through a portion of 6 are situated in the "Intolerable" quadrant, and the final quadrant encompasses zones 6 through 7, known as the "Acquisitions" quadrant. Each zone exhibits specific behaviors and characteristics.

<46>

As you familiarize yourself with each of these zones, try to recall instances in your own life when you found yourself in similar phases as you acquired new experiences and possessions.

The Zones defined:

Zone 1: Grateful: This zone marks the beginning of the newness model. It's when you have your new job, relationship, automobile, etc. A person is filled with bliss and excitement, experiencing a sense of pride for this fresh start.

Zone 2: Work/Life Contentment: This zone is where a person starts to grow comfortable with what they have received. It's considered non-threatening and has become a part of their everyday life. The initial newness may have worn off a bit, but the comfort remains prevalent.

Zone 3: View Into the Next Level: This zone is where individuals begin to envision a better version of their current life or possessions. This is the point in the model where some discomfort is introduced into their lives. Either the once-exciting thing or life is starting to show signs of wear, or there has been a major hiccup in performance.

Zone 4: Growth Begins: This zone is where a person stands at a crossroads, grappling with the discomfort and

<47>

the lack of knowledge on how to bridge the gap between where they are and where they want to be. The individual recognizes the desire for more but lacks the necessary resources.

Zone 5: Get Uncomfortable: This zone is when a person is determined to make a change and is motivated to do whatever it takes to achieve it. The individual returns to a state of humility and drive. They are humble enough to gather all the information needed to move forward and driven enough not to remain stagnant.

Zone 6: Bigger Than Current Place: This zone is where a person has acquired many of the skills or the knowledge needed to be ready for the next step or the newness. They have prepared themselves and are willing to let go of the old to make room for the new. They believe they deserve "this."

Zone 7: Seize Next Opportunity: This is the final zone within the model, and it's more of a formality in obtaining their "new." In this zone, a person is comfortable with the unknown. Anticipation is the prevailing emotion.

I still remember the day I bought my very first car all by myself. It was a time when I really needed a set of wheels to get around the city. Fresh out of school, life hadn't unfolded quite as I'd hoped. By day, I was work-

<48>

ing at a non-profit organization, and by night, I was scanning groceries at the local supermarket. Definitely not what I'd pictured after five years of studying to be an architect.

Instead of borrowing a car from my parents or anyone else, I decided to try and get one on my own. I stood in that dealership, determined to convince them I could handle the payments if they'd give me a shot. There was one guy who seemed to understand and said, "Let's see what we can find for you." In my mind, I just needed something with four wheels that ran smoothly, and an interior with working heat and air. Pretty basic, but that's where I was at the time.

After wandering around the lot for a couple of hours, I spotted a cute little white Dodge Neon with those distinctive bug-like headlights. It was used but looked well-maintained. I'm sure the dealer was relieved to see it go, but for me, it felt like I'd won a prize. That little car became my trusty companion, getting me where I needed to go until the day I realized I could aim for something even better. As I drove off the lot in my new white chariot, I was on cloud nine.

<49>

Adrian J.R. Davis

The Four Quadrants of Readiness:
The Bliss Quadrant:

During this phase, I was over the moon about my achievement. It was all I could think about. I snapped countless photos of the car and proudly showcased it to friends and family. I was so thrilled that I even shared the news with my pastor, referring to it as "my new blessing." To my astonishment, he generously contributed enough to cover my first three months of car payments. I was truly living in a state of bliss.

In this period, we delve into learning everything we can about what brings us joy, whether it's a person, a place, or a thing. If it's a new relationship, we pay attention to their moods, preferences, and habits—good days versus bad ones, favorite clothes, beloved foods, and so forth. While it might not turn out to be a lifelong partnership, sometimes it takes a while to realize that this person may not be the right fit. Often, it's only when we start feeling a bit uneasy in the relationship that we consider moving on. Surprisingly, studies show that even in painfully bad relationships, it can take up to seven attempts before someone finally musters the courage to leave.

So, what's the holdup? Why does it take so long? This scenario isn't limited to relationships—it applies to jobs too. Initially, a job might be a lifeline, putting food on the table and covering basic bills. But as time passes, the novelty fades, and our needs evolve.

<50>

Change only starts to become a consideration when that initial comfort diminishes and we become open to venturing into the unknown. This is when curiosity awakens, and we become aware of the possibility of something "better" or "newer."

The Awareness Quadrant:

Moving on from the Bliss Quadrant, we find ourselves in the Awareness Quadrant. This is when we start looking over the fence and see that there may be some "greener grass". We start to ask questions.

In the Awareness zone, we transition from comfort to discomfort and we start to realize how much we don't know about the next thing or phase in our lives. For those who have outgrown their job, they begin to look for more, new, and different. You become aware of things and people that start to really annoy you or make you uncomfortable.

People close to you might ask, "Didn't you love that job before? What changed?"

In most cases, the job or the environment did not change; you changed. You enjoyed all that you could enjoy and learned most of what you could learn in that environment, and now you "need" more. It moves from just being a want; you actually need to have a different environment or a new challenge. Otherwise, if you don't, you will start to become disengaged, bored, and shrink as a person or a professional.

<51>

As a side note, that is what I have seen in many of the organizations that I have consulted in when it comes to development and coaching. People are stuck in this zone. They are aware of better, but they don't know how to get there.

The shrinking of a person or a professional is a bad spiral to get into. Of course, no one knowingly seeks to get into this place, however, if you are not actively combating the shrinkage, then it could get you. Think about this, how many times have you had an awareness moment and you said to yourself, I should have been done with this job a long time ago, or I should have been out of this partnership a long time ago. The light bulb goes off. At that exact moment, you are not just going into the downward spiral into shrinkage, you are realizing that you have been there for some time. It is then you will embrace the uncomfortability and become a learner again for what is next for you on your life's journey.

The person that is at this level is now ready to move into:

The Intolerable Quadrant:

This zone is when you start to identify where you are and what you currently have and compare that to the place where you believe you should be. For example, you may come to the realization that $50,000, will no longer finance your livelihood. Maybe there has been a person added to your family, or maybe the kids are grow-

<52>

ing, or maybe the neighborhood is trending in a direction you are not satisfied with. It is then that you say, " I have to make more money so that we can feed these growing kids." Or "We gotta make more money to get another place in a different neighborhood.

Intolerable is not just a title; it is an attitude and an emotion. This will start to color your lense of how you see the world—the same world that you lived in six months ago, but your reality has changed. Because of that, your level of tolerance has been lowered. Now, what you were willing to accept in the past, bring you discomfort and agitation.

In this zone, you are the most uncomfortable, but are most open and eager to learn about how to get to the next level of comfort. This comfort can come in different shapes and sizes. Nevertheless, you will find out what it is and go after it.

I remember my family grew fast in a short amount of time. Our family of three was enjoying life and living in our little cottage for almost eleven years. Then came along our second child and things got a little tight, but there was no reason for panic. It was when baby number three, our beautiful princess, was announced to be on the way, that things got really uncomfortable really soon.

I can remember it like it was yesterday. I was sleep and enjoying a good night sleep and my wife, who seems to never sleep made enough noise to startle me and wake me from my slumber. I remember looking toward the

<53>

noise and I saw this silhouette standing in the doorway. It seemed like a scene from a movie, I swear there was smoke coming from the doorway or something. I was trying to adjust my eyes and see what was happening. I saw this shadow that looked like the silhouette of my wife standing in the doorway , but she was holding something. I was trying to figure out what it was. She then proceeded to flip on the light. It was then that I saw what was causing her to stand with an attitude that spoke volumes without her having to say a word. She was holding the pregnancy test that told us our fate as parents.

We had another one on the way! It had only been four or five months since the last one entered planet earth. I knew I had to start my expansion plan, if I had planned it or not. It was a necessity. This is what happens when you move from Awareness to Intolerable, you tend to learn at a rapid clip and push through whatever the uncomfortable level is.

For me, I remember walking in a daze for about a week. I truly could not believe what was happening. We had lived as a family of three for over 11 years and in a matter of two years we would be increasing our family by 66%. (that's just how my mind works). After shaking the dust off of my head and realizing this was not a dream, I had to commit to doing something, and I did.

My wife and I had talked about getting a new house for years. We had even talked about getting one built, this time things were different, and I was going to make

<54>

it happen. Sure enough, sparing you the details, within six months of our baby girl being born, we moved into our newly built house.

One thing to remember about the "intolerable" quadrant is that nothing will stand in your way of getting all of the information and the resources needed to be able to go after what you want. This is a stage that many people never get to. They may stay in zones three and four and may never go beyond that. After a while people who are stuck in those stages tend to sound like they are complaining because those who observe them, don't see them taking the next steps. A person who is intolerant looks like a person of action and a person of purpose.

Lastly, when a person is fed up with being uncomfortable and okay with the unknown, they move to:

The Acquisition Quadrant:

This is where a person knows what they want, knows how to get it and they are okay with the measures that they will have to take to acquire the new house, new car, new job , new relationship, etc. Fear is no longer the leading emotion in this person's life. It may still be there, but they are okay with doing "it" anyway.

So for that person who walks away from that job, those co-workers, and those benefits that they have had for years to pursue another one with the hope of a better experience, more fulfillment, and living on purpose, their mind is made up. Oftentimes this person may be as

<55>

happy as you have seen them in a long time. You may ask them, what are you going to do next, and they will smile with bliss and say: "I don't know, but I feel really good about this".

One major reason a person can feel so optimistic and lighthearted is that they know they have started to do the work and become bigger than their current place. If a person looks closely at them they will see that that person doesn't belong in that role, home, relationship, etc. anymore. The person in the Acquisition quadrant is just waiting for the right opportunity so that they can pounce. We have heard that luck happens when Opportunity and Preparations intersect.

I have seen people many times over decide to hire a coach or build a great relationship with a mentor and weeks later, things start to open up for them. Job opportunities arise or promotions or raises are offered suddenly. Is this a coincidence? I dare to say no. The preparation is now allowing the person who is getting ready for their "next" to be able to see opportunities much clearer.

Studies show that the Reticular Activation System (RAS) heightens what a person is most focused on and looks to attract into their lives. So when a person is ready, they are ultra-sensitive to the opportunities that are lurking. This is where a person is most ready to receive their new "Blessing", goal, or opportunity of a lifetime.

<56>

Recipe to Accelerate Your Readiness:

As stated at the very beginning of this chapter, we all want more, and we should. This is how we are created. If you would like to know how to accelerate your readiness to receive better things faster, then you will want to study the model carefully and identify where you are in the model.

Be honest with yourself and do not move to aspiration yet. In my book *Twice As Good In Half the Time*, I speak about why it is important to know where you currently are in life. If you really want to know where you are in the model and framework, you will want to properly assess where you are.

After honestly identifying where you are, you can make a plan to get you to the next zone. For example, if you are in Zone Two in your life with your job, understand that you will have to explore more to be able to increase the discomfort in your world. I know this sounds counter intuitive, but it will be the thing that heats your seat and makes you want to move.

It has been said that: "It is not until the pain of where you are is more uncomfortable than the fear of where you are going, that you will make a change". In

<57>

essence, you get to determine how quickly you move to your next iconic moment in your life.

<58>

VALUE CREATION

Unleashing Impact and Influence in the World

Companies hire people primarily because they have the skills for the job, but true change-makers create value.

Before Oprah became the renowned queen of daytime TV, she worked at CBS and ABC news affiliates in Nashville and Baltimore. Howard Schultz managed coffee machines for a company called Hammarplast before leading Starbucks and becoming its CEO. Colonel Sanders, the fried chicken legend, was once a train conductor.

Remember, while your job can be a platform for amazing things, it's your unique ideas and the value you bring to a specific audience that can change the world. Your impact and success are determined by the value you offer to the market.

We talked about Oprah Winfrey, Howard Schultz, and Colonel Sanders. They all had regular jobs before making it big. They honed their skills within those jobs. Like them, when you decide you want to serve a broader audience and make a bigger impact, you'll need to learn the skill of scaling.

Scaling means taking something small and making it available to a much larger group. Many people struggle with this skill, so they only reach a small audience.

Let me be clear: I'm not suggesting you shouldn't work for someone else. I'm saying, consider the impact

<59>

you're making. The harder it is to replace you and your impact, the more valuable you are. Think about it: can you perform brain surgery right now? Can you effectively lead a company of five thousand, aiming for a seven to ten percent increase in profits each year?

If you said no to either of those, you understand the concept of value. It might be because you don't want the pressure of so many people relying on you, or perhaps you don't have the expertise to handle such crucial responsibilities. But those are just two examples. There are many roles out there that impact even more lives on a larger scale than our current positions.

We've touched on what makes you valuable, but let's dive into how to become valuable. If you've been wondering how to achieve that, you're thinking big, and that's commendable.

Some folks believe that the only path to success is through college or university. While I have a different perspective, let's go with this idea for now. Success comes in various forms, and it's reflected in the value you bring to the world. If attending college is what you need to gain the skills and knowledge, then go for it. However, keep in mind that life itself can be your greatest teacher.

"Life Is College:

Back when I was getting ready for the University of Tennessee at Knoxville, I had to do some prep work. I

<60>

had to choose my major, pick my electives, and decide where I'd stay on campus. It strikes me that the same process applies when you're getting ready for the College of Life. You've got to take charge and figure out what you really want to do in life, and then find out what skills or know-how you need to be ready.

Lots of folks pour tons of energy into learning their craft in college, but only give a fraction of that effort to learning the ropes in 'real life' and applying what's necessary to excel in their field or in life. According to a blog article titled 'How Many People Use Their Degrees in 2023?' from The Small Business Blog, only 27.3% of college grads actually end up working in the field they studied for in college. To go even further, 34% of those who do end up in their field of study could've gotten the job without a degree.

We can see this in two ways: either people aren't getting the tools they need to succeed in life from what they learn in college, or we need to keep on learning skills long after college, even if it's not in our field of study. Remember, we're not just talking about getting a paycheck; we're talking about adding value, about making a real impact, not just going home and watching TV.

So, if you really want to make your way through life's college, you've got to put in the effort to figure out what classes you need to take to be successful. But what does that look like, you might wonder? Well, here's an idea:

<61>

1. Decide what you want to do in life.
2. Figure out what skills you need to step into that field or industry.
3. Study hard, give it your all."

Find out what you want to do in Life:

"Similar to choosing a major in college, you'll want to decide what you want to do in life. But unlike college, it's important to think about how you want to make a positive impact on others. This goes beyond just getting a job or earning a paycheck; it's about contributing something meaningful to your field or industry. Often, this drive comes from a personal experience that ignites a passion to work in that area. It could be a promise to oneself after a tough situation or loss.

The best reason to pursue anything is because you truly love it. Imagine feeling a sense of fulfillment from providing a service or seeing the impact of your work on others. It's like a rush of happiness when you're in your element. You become hooked on the smiles, the 'aha' moments, and the heartfelt feedback that comes your way. If you haven't felt this before, it might mean you haven't yet discovered your true calling.

Next, figure out the skills you need to excel in your chosen field or industry. Once you've identified your passion, become a pro in that arena. Strive to be in the top 5%-10% of what you do. It's perfectly fine to declare, 'I want to be the best,' but be ready to back it up.

<62>

This is where 'life's university' comes into play. Unlike traditional universities, there's no set curriculum or someone telling you which classes to take to meet a certain hour requirement for graduation. You're in charge of gathering the skills you need, and you get to choose your mentors along the way. How long you study a topic is up to you and when you feel you've truly mastered it. Don't get hung up on arbitrary numbers like 10,000 hours or a specific number of repetitions. Learning happens when it happens.

Choosing the right mentor can greatly impact your proficiency and the time it takes to master a subject. A skilled mentor will be honest about whether they're the best fit for you and what you need to progress. If they are the right fit, they'll expect you to take their guidance seriously, completing assignments or tasks they assign. When you find that mentor, absorb as much as you can from them.

Throughout history, transformative figures have had mentors who taught them invaluable lessons. The bond between pupil and mentor becomes unbreakable. For instance, Bob Proctor had Earl Nightingale, Napoleon Hill had Andrew Carnegie, Les Brown had Mike Williams, Richard Branson had Sir Freddie Laker, Tony Robbins had Jim Rohn, and I have had mentors like Derek Young, Dewayne Scott, Bishop Jerry L. Maynard, Mike Emkes, and Dr. James (Jim) Irvine. This matters because a mentor continues to impart new skills, often demonstrating

<63>

them in real-time, which is a powerful part of the learning process."

What skills do you need:

"Previously, I mentioned having several mentors, and I want to emphasize that having multiple mentors is a valuable approach. In fact, I believe it should be encouraged. You're a multi-dimensional person, and relying on one mentor or professor alone may not cover all your needs. When students attend colleges or universities, they don't stick with just one professor throughout their entire freshman year. They also don't rely on just one person to teach them everything about a subject. Some individuals excel in specific areas, so it's important to absorb their expertise and wisdom in those domains. But also, be open to seeking guidance from others who have specialized skills related to that subject.

At the same time, as you consider who should be your mentor or resource, think about what you already know. While you won't know everything (that's what the mentor/professor is for), coming with a foundation will greatly benefit your learning journey. It's like multiplication - anything multiplied by zero is still zero. If you come in with nothing, you won't make much progress. So, having a starting point in mind is crucial. From personal experience, I've found that 'professors' value their time and don't appreciate it being wasted.

For instance, when I pursued a career in architecture,

<64>

I understood the basics I needed to grasp: math, science, and art. These formed the foundation, and I sought out professors who could teach me in these core areas. During my first year in the college of architecture, I not only took those essential classes but also discovered other subjects I hadn't initially considered.

I share this to illustrate that if you have a starting point for the things you believe you need guidance on, you'll often receive that and more. Let's say you're seeking advice on how to increase your income. Your mentor might offer practical strategies, but they might also delve into deeper aspects that influence your financial situation. Be receptive to their guidance and remember, you're learning because you don't have all the answers yet."

Study Like Heck:

"Finally, when you've found your mentor in life and they're sharing their wisdom and experiences with you, it's crucial to take their advice seriously and delve into the concepts and tools they provide–study like your life depends upon it, because in some respects it does. I remember a conversation I had with a wise businessman in my early thirties. I was a bit nervous about speaking with him, feeling somewhat intimidated. He reassured me by expressing how much he gained from passing down knowledge to the next generation. But he also added, 'I don't want to waste my time; I want to see you put what I share with you into action.' That made me realize the im-

<65>

portance of paying attention and executing the plans we discussed.

In life, your learning should be divided into two main categories: Application in Real Life and Verification through Theory. While you receive valuable insights from your mentors, it's essential to validate this information with reliable sources. Any worthwhile mentor will be able to support their ideas with solid data or research.

One of my mentors introduced me to the concept of 'Johari's Window' when we were discussing emotional intelligence. After our meeting, I eagerly researched it and found that not only was he spot on, but it also aligned perfectly with what I needed. This framework, created by psychologists in 1955, had never crossed my path before. It was entirely new to me. Yet, it helped me start identifying blind spots in my life and seek help in areas where I couldn't see clearly.

This is why it's crucial to listen to your mentors, study their teachings, and then put them into practice. There are so many aspects of life we haven't yet discovered, and with a willingness to shift our mindset, we can grow immensely.

After absorbing and studying the newfound wisdom, it's time to take action. This is where value addition begins. If you're employed, you apply what you've learned from your mentor to your job, aligning it with what your role requires. This is the phase where people distinguish themselves in terms of productivity, success, and charac-

<66>

ter. They don't just do the bare minimum; they enhance it. They integrate the lessons from someone who's been down that path into their current role, making them more valuable.

Consider two employees: one who comes in at 9 am and leaves at 4:30 pm, doing exactly what's asked of them, and another who goes the extra mile, coming in early and leaving late. Is the first employee a bad worker? Not necessarily. However, in the competitive job market, everything is compared. So, while the first employee isn't doing anything wrong, compared to the second, who has a mentor emphasizing the value of going above and beyond, they may seem to be falling short.

Is this comparison fair? It's hard to say. But fairness isn't always the benchmark. If you were running a company, and you had an employee who was only doing what was expected versus one who was going above and beyond, who would catch your attention? This is why putting your mentor's advice into practice can be the difference between standing out and blending into the crowd of mediocrity."

7 Steps to Value Creation

This model has proven successful in various settings, from corporate America and small businesses to multi-level marketing and faith-based organizations. While I wouldn't quite call it a Universal law, it comes pretty close.

<67>

These steps have guided many individuals I've coached over the years to advance in their careers, rise in their industries, and even increase their earnings. The process is easy to grasp, but the devil is in the details.

Before we dive into it, let's define 'value':

- Value Creation: The process of using labor and resources to create something that fulfills the needs of others. – Digital Resource

- It involves producing goods or offering services that customers consistently find valuable, forming a bond of loyalty. -Deskera.com

The first definition is applicable in the workplace, your job, or your 9-5. The second definition is more commonly embraced by entrepreneurs seeking to add value in the marketplace. We'll revisit these definitions as we unpack the stages of Value Creation.

1. Understand the Job Description:

Absolutely, understanding both the written and unspoken job expectations is essential for success in any role, whether it's your first job or your last before retirement. It's like a mutual agreement between you and the organization or the people you work for. This clarity ensures that, at the very least, you'll meet the expectations set by your client or employer.

In most cases, there are two job descriptions: the one that's officially written down, and the one that's understood but not explicitly stated. The written description is

<68>

what you typically find on the company's website or job listings. However, it's important to note that this description may be outdated and tailored for the previous employee.

It's common for hiring managers to get accustomed to the performance of the previous employee, which then leads to the creation of an unspoken job description. For example, if a job officially requires eight daily tasks, but the previous employee consistently completed only six, and the boss was content with this, then the unspoken agreement becomes six tasks. When a new hire looks at the written job description, they may feel overwhelmed, not realizing that the boss actually expects only six of those tasks.

Similarly, if the previous employee regularly completed ten tasks, even though the official description listed eight, the boss gets used to this higher output. This can lead to potential disillusionment for new hires or transfers from other departments, especially if the job description hasn't been updated. The boss's expectation remains at ten tasks, even though it wasn't communicated beforehand.

In the first scenario, where the boss is accustomed to six out of eight tasks daily, someone who completes all eight tasks is seen as an overachiever. Conversely, in the second scenario, a person who completes the tasks outlined in the written description might be viewed as not fitting the job. That's why it's crucial to have a clear un-

<69>

derstanding of both the written and unspoken job expectations.

2. Learn the Job:

After understanding your role, it's important to focus on how you execute it. This is where your curiosity and courage come into play. I want to emphasize that this step should be about learning, not immediate performance. While it's natural to aspire to greatness, this phase is dedicated to the process of learning, which is a crucial part of achieving greatness.

Whatever your position, strive to master it thoroughly. Aim to become an expert in what you do. You want people to say, "If you have questions about 'x', you have to reach out to (your name)." If you haven't started hearing this yet, it means you haven't become a Subject Matter Expert (SME) in your office, company, or industry.

In your learning journey, utilize all available resources and gather as much information as you can. It's not out of the question to observe how your company operates and then compare it with your competitors. This serves two purposes: understanding your competition and identifying if there's a more efficient or innovative approach to achieve the same result.

In life, we are rewarded for efficiency and innovation. I recall taking on a role with a large international organization, responsible for creating and guiding leaders

<70>

through a six-month learning program. The first six months were everything I had envisioned. I traveled monthly to different locations with the leadership program, gaining insights into various business units in North America. I understood the production processes at each location, and my boss and I were aligned on my responsibilities. However, when COVID-19 emerged, everything changed.

Suddenly, we couldn't physically travel to all the locations, and I had to find a way to continue learning about them in the workplace landscape. I began consulting colleagues and researching how they were handling similar situations in their organizations. My curiosity was on overdrive because I needed to figure out 'how' I was going to excel in my role.

While your situation may not be as extreme, many departments have a "how-to" guide or a procedure manual. If not, you'll need to be a bit of a detective, getting curious about what needs to be done, how, and when. This is the essence of truly learning your job.

Lastly, give yourself the time required to learn. Avoid being distracted by shiny new things. Focus on excelling in this step because it's a crucial foundation for the next phase.

3. Look for Gaps

Once you've thoroughly learned about your role or the space you're in within the marketplace, it's time to

<71>

shift your focus. Your aim now is not just to gather information about the job, but to identify potential improvements in the job, the tasks, or the processes involved. This is where true value creation happens, and it involves this step and the next.

Before we dive into identifying gaps, let me emphasize why the next two steps are challenging. Looking for gaps requires a keen eye to pinpoint areas where you can create the most value for your department, organization, or industry. It demands effort and the ability to see beyond the everyday routine. Just because someone told you "this is how it's done" doesn't mean it's the most effective way. Those who have the patience and skill to critically examine processes and procedures often drive innovation and disrupt the status quo.

However, it's crucial to remember that you can't stop at identifying gaps; you must also proceed to the next step. Otherwise, you're merely pointing out problems without offering solutions. Think about how many people in history wanted to travel faster than by foot. Many may have voiced their desire for a better way, but how many took action?

In 3000 BC, the early Mesopotamians made the groundbreaking innovation of the wheel. Wealthy individuals of that time got to experience this luxury. The covered wagon came along later in 1717, brought to the US by German immigrants. Those transitioning from direct horseback riding to the covered wagon likely

<72>

thought they had hit the jackpot of innovations. I won't delve into the entire evolution of transportation, but I challenge you to consider what our ancestors would say if they witnessed our current modes of transportation. If you could go back in time and tell them about electric cars, they might not believe you. The gap in technology and innovation would likely be too vast for them to grasp.

This brings us back to identifying gaps in processes, systems, or work methods. When seeking to improve long-standing practices, you must identify a gap that can be clearly communicated to those affected by it. If the gap is too revolutionary and cannot be effectively communicated, your chances of success diminish significantly.

To illustrate, I once worked for my mother's nonprofit organization right out of school. The organization aimed to help people acquire homes and prevent foreclosure or mortgage issues for homeowners. As I worked for the organization over the years, I noticed opportunities for improving how we served our clients. My mother was open to continuous improvement, and one day I proposed a "big idea": transitioning our services to a virtual and electronic format.

This would allow clients to complete their intake paperwork at home. Additionally, it would enable us to schedule more clients and already have a good understanding of their situation when they visited the office.

<73>

This small innovation led to significant positive outcomes.

I continued to seek ways to innovate and automate in other aspects of our business. I explored how we conducted counseling sessions, which could have been quite revolutionary in the early 2000s. I envisioned using Skype for video chat or virtual counseling. However, the world I was working in wasn't ready for it at the time. I set up a location in the local mall to introduce this concept, but people weren't ready to embrace it. The government organization we were associated with wasn't prepared to endorse this type of counseling either. I was out on a limb of innovation by myself. Why? Because I didn't make the innovation gap smaller. I introduced a huge technological leap to a process that had primarily been face-to-face. I didn't do a sufficient job of explaining the why and the how of this new mode of communication and private counseling, so people weren't ready for it. That idea, for that business, mostly remained just an idea.

Twenty years later, virtual meetings and working from home are the norm, and people prefer it. Identifying the gap doesn't just mean pointing out problems or weaknesses; it's about evaluating how much that gap is hindering progress, impacting an industry, or preventing a group of people from reaching a desired goal. Understanding these gaps will help you or your team effectively communicate why attention or possibly innovation is needed in that area.

<74>

One last thing about looking for gaps: you're not being negative by doing this. In fact, you have to present yourself as the opposite to the people you're bringing this to. There has to be a balance of highlighting problems while also suggesting solutions. If you only share problems without offering solutions, you may be labeled as negative or a problem-bringer.

When presenting a gap, be prepared to connect the next step to your delivery. If there were an ideal way to identify a gap, it would be to share with those who have the authority to make changes, approach the situation with positivity, view it as an opportunity to enhance or address a problem, and finally, express your willingness to be part of the solution process.

4. Solve the Problem

This step in creating value should be approached with flexibility and a willingness to invest your own time, potentially outside of regular work hours or away from your primary responsibilities. For instance, if you're working for a company and notice a data collection problem, even if it's not part of your main role, be prepared to dedicate extra time during your lunch break or after work to explore potential solutions.

Reflecting on my previous experience at my mother's non-profit organization, I pursued improvements during separate dedicated times, rather than while I was counseling clients.

<75>

While solving the problem or exploring solutions, it's important to keep in mind how this will benefit and who it will benefit. The more closely you align your thinking with these considerations, the easier it will be to articulate and advocate for the new innovation.

Another aspect to consider in problem-solving is pacing yourself. Understand that many established practices and procedures have been in place for a considerable time. Finding a solution might come in incremental steps before you arrive at a completely revised approach.

You may encounter situations where a particular process seems entirely unnecessary to you. However, remember that when that process was established, someone or a group of people believed it was the best way at the time. Your proposed new approach may come as a surprise or a welcome change to those affected. Just ensure that your proposed change isn't so drastic that it jeopardizes the business's stability.

In the context of value creation, it's important to acknowledge that innovation often requires collaboration. When seeking to innovate, it's crucial that you and your team keep the details of the new idea confidential until you're ready to move forward. If there isn't alignment regarding the timing and release of this information, it could lead to confusion and counteract the value creation process.

<76>

5. Communicate the Solution:

Once you've discovered a solution and confirmed its effectiveness through repeated testing, it's time to share it with others. It's crucial to identify the right audience for your solution. Think of this as recognizing the stakeholders - those who have a vested interest in what you're offering. Stakeholders can take different forms, but they are most commonly leaders of organizations or departments, customers of your product or service, and individuals like yourself who use a process or system that could benefit from your innovation.

Leaders: I've found a lot of success in the corporate world by adding value to leaders of departments and organizations. There were times when I wasn't at the desired level of employment, but I knew I could get there with a few improvements and positive changes. I learned early on that if I could solve problems and help streamline operations, reduce costs, or boost revenue, leadership would start to take notice.

Customers: Most people prefer simplicity and ease of use. When working with this group of stakeholders, I crafted messages that were quick, detailed, and thorough. While I won't go into too much detail here, I believe in tailoring your sales approach to how people want to buy. Essentially, this means understanding their preferred method of purchasing. If you can present your product or service in a way that aligns with their preferences, they're more likely to buy in quickly and potentially become ad-

<77>

vocates for your idea or product. Some clients prefer a swift approach, so you'll need to deliver promptly. For those who want a thorough understanding, having data on what was and what could be will satisfy them.

Current Users: Lastly, consider those who are in a similar position to you. They might be doing the exact same job in a different organization within the same industry. If you can demonstrate how your improvements save time, boost productivity, and potentially increase revenue, you'll enhance your value to this group of stakeholders.

I recall a conference in Cincinnati, OH at the Duke Energy Center during my thriving time with a non-profit organization. I had just transitioned the organization from a paper-based system to an automated one. Word spread quickly about the new innovation and the many benefits it brought to our company.

I vividly remember an organization from Texas, doing the exact same thing we did, whose executive director asked if I'd be willing to visit and share how I accomplished it. Back then, I didn't realize the value I'd created in the marketplace, but now I understand that she was saying, "You've made a significant impact, and I'd be willing to cover your travel and accommodation expenses if you'd spend a few hours showing us how you improved a process/system we've had in place for years."

Once you've determined which stakeholders you'll be sharing your new idea with, it's essential to figure out

<78>

the best way to communicate the improvement. You can do this through showing or telling. Showing methods consists of two processes:

Stacking:

When it comes to "Stacking," you'll demonstrate the existing product, service, or process and then showcase how the new method complements the old one. This approach allows those who are accustomed to the current way to understand that you're not getting rid of it, but rather enhancing it for improvement.

Replacing:

On the other hand, "Replace the old" means illustrating to stakeholders how the current approach hasn't been providing them with the optimal results it could. You'll explain why replacing this method will yield better outcomes in the same amount of time or even less. This way, they can see the potential for improvement.

Telling methods:

When it comes to the "Telling" method, it's designed for individuals who prefer to absorb information through listening. They may enjoy it on a podcast or catching a concise presentation at a conference or seminar. Regardless of the medium, it's crucial to be thorough in your choice of words and vividly depict the contrast between the current state and the potential future.

<79>

Mastering the skill of making people excited about the impending reality is one of the key strengths you possess after identifying the gap and devising the solution. You must articulate it in a way that ignites desire. I'd even go as far as to say they should feel they absolutely need it. When someone believes they need something, they'll go to great lengths to acquire it.

Consider this: If someone were to convince the world of a weight-loss pill today that was both safe and controllable, requiring no exercise and allowing you to eat as you please, how many would go to great lengths to obtain it? A considerable number! They'd weigh the discomfort of working out and the challenge of maintaining a strict diet against the perceived benefits of the pill.

Finally, if you were able to announce that this pill was exclusively produced by your internal team and it was the only source, the value you've created would skyrocket. People would go to extraordinary lengths to acquire what you're offering. However, it all starts with effectively communicating the solution.

6. Negotiate Your Terms

In negotiating your terms, you want to be very careful not to put yourself in a precarious position. You want to make sure you are in control of the outcome. Before you go into the negotiation with your employer, client, or anyone else, you want to decide what you will accept and what you will definitely not accept from this conversa-

<80>

tion with the person you are negotiating with.

You want to enter that meeting or series of meetings with the mindset of: "If I don't get this, then nothing changes and I take my idea, solution, or improvement somewhere else to be valued at the level that I believe it deserves. Never do the following things: Be undersold, settle, or forget your value.

Don't be undersold. This could manifest as someone in the workplace saying, "Thank you for your innovative idea; we will put your name in a drawing for an award at the end of the year." Later, you find out that the company implemented your idea or new product and either saved the company millions of dollars or made the company millions of dollars. The best you will get out of that is an award, if you are chosen.

Now, I can hear some people saying, "Wait a minute, are you telling me I should be selling all of my innovative ideas instead of bringing them to the workplace?" Remember how I started this section: you must control the outcome. If, for some reason, all a person wants to get out of this new improvement they are bringing to the company is an award, then great, they got what they wanted. If not, however, this is where many folks run into problems. They learn of the benefits the company or a client is getting from their improvement and go on to say things like: "I came up with that idea," or "They pretty much stole that from me," or "I can't believe I just

<81>

got a trophy from this improvement when the company is going to benefit greatly from my idea." This is a clear sign that the person did not intend for the negotiation to end like that. They feel like they got the short end of the deal and they are disappointed.

Why feel that way when you can come to the table knowing this is what I am looking for in exchange for something that will increase your productivity, reduce your downtime, create a better process, etc.? Think about it this way: if it were a vendor coming to the organization to sell them something that could improve their outputs or outcomes, and the company made a decision to purchase that item, how much would they be willing to pay for it? I am not telling you to request that much of a raise or a bonus, but you should aim for something that you will be comfortable with as you go into the office every day.

For those serving as individual consultants and seeking to bring something to the marketplace, it's crucial to thoroughly study your market. Understand that if your improvement is novel and impactful enough, you may find early adopters willing to invest at a higher price point initially. Later on, you can work on attracting late-comers at a lower rate, but do not undersell yourself.

Don't Settle: Settling can manifest in various ways. You might grow weary, tired of trying to convey the value of what you're offering, exhausted from hearing rejections, and disillusioned when the vision in your

<82>

mind's eye doesn't materialize. My advice to you is to do your best to persevere. Think about historical figures like Thomas Edison and Colonel Sanders who faced consistent rejection. Initially, they envisioned a better world and industry, but their reality didn't align. If they had settled for what others said or the rejection they received, we might never have had Colonel's Chicken Recipe, the light bulb, or countless other innovations.

Another form of settling is not being prepared with a clear picture of what you want in exchange for your value addition. This could be a raise, a bonus, a promotion for those in a traditional job, or for those not in a 9-5, it might be a specified contract amount or a share of ownership. The possibilities are endless. The key is to know what you're seeking in exchange for what you're about to offer the organization, the industry, or the world at large.

I recall reading that in an effort to sustain the business, Facebook CEO Mark Zuckerberg took only one dollar as a salary for an entire year, ensuring his team was paid and the organization ran smoothly. He did this with confidence because he knew what he would gain in return for that year, understanding the company's prospectus. He ensured his shares in the company were secure and that he would receive his share on the backend through dividends when times improved.

Knowing your baseline acceptance level will guide you in discerning when the conversation is headed in the

<83>

right direction or when it's time to exit. For instance, if you've demonstrated your suitability for the next level and aim to introduce a more effective process to replace an outdated one, seeking a promotion might be in order. If leadership doesn't align with this direction, graciously thank them for their time and initiate your exit strategy.

You needn't make a scene, but at the same time, ensure you don't give away the new process, system, or improvement you were planning to provide.

From one perspective, it may appear unfavorable, but remember that you are your brand, and you do possess value. It's essential to calculate the value you bring to the table throughout your career journey. This leads me to the final aspect of negotiation: knowing your value.

Know your value: I once had someone who had known me for years and had witnessed my career and life progress ask me a question: "Do you still offer $50 coaching sessions?" I genuinely smiled and replied, "No, I no longer have anything on my development slate priced at $50."

This individual remembered me from a time when I conducted one-hour coaching sessions, and apparently, I wasn't worth fifty dollars to them back then. As they recognized that I was achieving more significant things and positively impacting more lives, they wanted to revert to the previously discussed price point. I wasn't offended; I simply needed to convey that my value had risen, and my

<84>

previous pricing was no longer applicable. If they wanted to achieve real, immediate, life-changing results, they might want to consider my current pricing because it could change soon. As I continue to learn and enhance my skills to be even more effective, that's precisely what will happen.

You must understand your value and not be swayed by anything or anyone attempting to diminish your worth in the marketplace. Once again, consider the negotiation process from this perspective: the person purchasing a product or service is seeking a great deal, just as much as the person selling or offering something novel. With that in mind, for you to feel like you've achieved your desired outcome in a transaction, you need to establish a baseline for what you will accept in exchange for what you're offering. This baseline represents one side of your value zone. There's also an upper limit to your value zone. While most people might not want to acknowledge it and would prefer to be paid as much as possible, the issue with that is if the other party overpays, they may lose trust in you or your brand. This could potentially harm your relationship with someone or a company that you could have had a long-lasting partnership with.

This action and due diligence requires discipline. Give more than you take In the words of Wallace D. Wattles, author of the *Science of Getting Rich*: "Give to people more in used value than you take from them in cash value. Then you are adding to the life of the world

<85>

with every business transaction." In simple terms, ensure that what you're presenting provides sustained benefits far beyond the agreed-upon price. The only way to achieve this is through careful calculation.

Consider the price of gum, which typically ranges from $1 to $5 per pack. Can you imagine paying $500 for a pack of 10 sticks of gum? It sounds absurd. Why does it seem so outlandish? It's because the perceived value of ten sticks of gum to one person doesn't justify that price. They can extol its freshness and mintiness all day, but no one will believe it will add $500 worth of satisfaction and change to their life.

Conversely, stumbling upon a four-year-old car with only 15,000 miles on the speedometer listed for $500 would feel like a steal. You'd probably ask the salesperson, "Excuse me, is this $500 a month, because surely you can't be selling this for that amount outright."

Internally, we all have a range, and it's crucial to understand that range in the marketplace and be able to negotiate it when presenting our new value proposition to those we are engaging with. The person who knows their range the best exudes confidence and can provide a justifiable reason for such a significant improvement. Knowing your range also empowers you to peacefully walk away from an agreement that makes you uncomfortable.

Finally, when you've determined the worth of yourself and/or your new improvement, be ready to discuss all the benefits with the stakeholder, but refrain from di-

<86>

vulging the entire idea. You shouldn't reveal the secret sauce until both parties have agreed on the terms of the transaction. This could involve a new role within an organization, a promotion, a newly established client/ consultant relationship, and so on. Regardless, when your stakeholder realizes they can't do without you or your new improvement and they propose their offering for it, it's your turn to claim the reward if it falls within your value zone.

<87>

7. Acquire Your Reward:

This final step may seem straightforward enough: get what you've negotiated and deliver what you've pitched. Ideally, having everything in writing at this point is preferred. However, in an organizational setting, it can get a bit tricky. This is where your situational awareness comes into play - knowing when to assert yourself if what was agreed upon isn't being implemented.

For instance, let's say you and your boss met with their superior, and you've come up with a more efficient way to produce widgets that will boost productivity and income. They agreed to let you have your own team to implement this. Now, it's crucial to keep an eye on the calendar and the organizational environment.

If it's been three weeks since that conversation, consider stopping by your boss's office and inquire, "Hey boss, I was just checking in to see how the new team formation is coming along. Is there anything you need from me?" A boss with a decent level of emotional intelligence and awareness should be able to update you on the status of the team formation.

Ensure that you're prepared when the stakeholder sets an implementation date on the calendar. It's showtime, and now you must ensure that what you discovered back in the early stages of value creation is showcased for everyone to see.

<88>

Remember, the better you perform in this new role, the more expansive the opportunities will become as you continue to ascend the value creation ladder.

<89>

The Recipe:

Ensure you have a deep understanding of your job and earn the trust of your leadership or industry peers before actively seeking out areas for improvement.

Once you've established credibility with your team, boss and your stakeholders, start identifying potential enhancements.

Dedicate your personal time, outside of regular work or obligations, to diligently uncover and address these gaps.

Once you've devised your innovative approach for the market, begin by highlighting the surface-level benefits and potential solutions.

When you find someone willing to put their trust in you and your new approach, go the extra mile to add value to their experience.

Don't be surprised if others start showing a keen interest in what you're doing and seek you out for your expertise.

<90>

MOMENTUM

Newton's First Law of Motion states that a body at rest will remain at rest unless an outside force acts on it. Similarly, if you find yourself not progressing toward your desired destination, it may be because you're coasting along at a steady pace, frequency, or intensity. It's a signal that you need a change in your life.

We've discussed the profound influence of community on your identity and actions, albeit briefly in the chapter on the result pyramid. In this chapter, we'll delve much deeper into how circumstances materialize for you, even when the outcomes aren't to your liking.

It's a fundamental truth that everyone is, in fact, attaining precisely what they truly desire. While they may not be content with the end results they've attracted, it doesn't alter the fundamental law governing how things manifest.

In the ancient text known as the "Bible," there's a scripture that resonates: "Whatsoever things ye desire, when ye pray, believe that ye receive them, and ye shall have them" (Mark 11:24, KJV). In essence, this passage conveys that if you deeply desire something and invest strong emotions into that desire, it will materialize in your life. What's truly remarkable about this scripture and concept is that many people perceive prayer as a singular event. However, it's better understood as a continu-

<91>

ous mode of thinking and communicating in a meta-physical manner.

In reality, praying could be viewed as articulating the deepest desires of your heart while attaching genuine emotions to them. Objectively speaking, it matters less what you initially think and later verbalize. If you consistently focus on it, imbued with enough emotion, you will inevitably draw it closer to you. This perspective sheds light on why certain things may have manifested in your life, even if you express ambivalence about receiving them.

Let's say it's winter and you start thinking about the cold and flu season. You might say things like, "I don't want to get sick" or "I can't afford to get a cold." When you focus on sickness, you might unknowingly attract situations that make you more likely to catch a virus, even if you're taking precautions like medicine or getting a flu shot.

This is also why some people who don't pay much attention to news about how many people are getting sick or what virus is going around tend to stay healthy, while others get sick more often. We'll talk more about this later.

Remember, in the same book that talks about believing and receiving, it also says, "What I was afraid of has come upon me" (Job 3:25, KJV).

The important thing to know is that this law works, whether you like it or not. You have to focus on what

<92>

you really want and not just think about things you don't want because of what's happening around you. Building momentum means consistently thinking about what's good for you, and over time, you'll start to see those good things happen in your life.

Your Thoughts Create Your Reality:

Your actions and your state of mind have the power to attract people and opportunities into your life. When you focus your thoughts on what you want, you increase the likelihood of achieving it. Let's keep this practical. Have you ever decided to do something even when you didn't know how you'd do it at first? But somehow, all of the pieces of the puzzle came together and allowed you to accomplish your goal. That was an example of your thoughts creating your reality.

I can recall when I was in my early thirties, I had this idea that it would be cool to run a half marathon. Now, the first hurdle was that I had never run long distances. I was more into "sprinting sports". I enjoyed games where there were short bursts of running and stopping, like football and basketball. Another potential problem was that right after I decided to start training, I ended up twisting my ankle.

After a visit to the doctor and getting the green light to resume training, I just started running. Technically, I didn't have a clue what I was doing; I just put one foot in front of the other. For the initial weeks, I couldn't run a

<93>

full mile without stopping. And when I got close to a mile, I'd get a cramp in the oddest place - my ribcage. But I kept at it every day.

It was winter, so the days were shorter and it was dark by the time I started my run. In my mind, the only thing I could see in front of me was a picture of myself lining up to run thirteen and a half miles and finishing it.

Once I got my stamina up to running one and a half miles without stopping, I faced another challenge. I would get these terrible chills right after I finished running. I thought, maybe this is a sign that I'm not meant to do this. But instead of quitting, I researched why I was getting the chills and how I could stop them. I found out that I could not get my heart rate up so high and then just stop. This is a term called "Exertional Heat Illness". It was an internal mechanism to make sure that I did not overheat. So I learned that I had to slowly cool my muscles down instead of abruptly stopping. Because I had never run or practiced running this long, this was not something I knew, nor did I need to know.

I didn't go into my goal with an alphabetized instruction booklet: "I'm having chills, let's look in the C section for chills." The journey to achievement will be full of challenges that you have never experienced. However, you grow from every challenge you endure and learn how to handle them in the future. I learned how to eat before and after a run. I learned the proper shoes I needed and the proper shoe size for running 13.1 miles.

<94>

And even after I achieved my goal and ran the half marathon, I had another lesson: Your toenail will die and fall off. Ouch!

So, if you say you want to visit one of the seven wonders of the world, set your mind to it and think in that direction, only! Don't give space to thoughts like "what if I can't make it happen." That thought alone has a direction.

Momentum is driven by constant forward movement. Think of the image of a snowball. In its initial form, it may be as small as a balled-up sock. If you push that small snowball down the hill, it won't start off very fast. However, as it continues to move, it will start picking up more snow and other particles with it as it grows in size and speed. After a while, the sock-size snowball has turned into something big and has taken a life of its own. It no longer needs a push because the mass x velocity has taken over.

The same thing happens with your thoughts. The one small thought of doubt you accept starts as sock-size, but if you keep revisiting that thought, it starts to pick up things that validate its position. So what you doubted initially starts to turn into a real belief, and once that happens, it is hard to stop the spiraling.

That is why that scripture I used in the opening said, "what you believe you receive and then you have." The snowball turns into a snow boulder, and they don't stop so easily. A snowball of pessimism will turn into a boul-

<95>

der of failure because as it rolls, it is attracting everything it needs to achieve its pessimistic outcome. Here is the even trickier part to this: It is almost impossible to tell a person who is experiencing these negative results anything different than what they are experiencing. Even though they don't like the results, they are creating them. Arguing with them is a waste of time and energy because their reality has shown them what they need to be in that reality.

Think about this, forty degrees is just what it is, a temperature. If you have someone from a warm region and someone from a cold region experience that forty-degree day, the one from the warmer region will be looking for more clothes and blankets to stay warm, while the person from the cooler region may be sitting in shorts and flip-flops. The climate did not change, but the way the two individuals have experienced weather and thought about weather controls their perspective on it.

I remember I was taking my kids out on the streets of my neighborhood one year for the Halloween tradition of Trick or Treating. Now, when I grew up, it was mostly cold on the 31st of October. For some reason this year, it was, to me, sweater weather, but not cold, to say the least.

My kids and I walked through the neighborhood and encountered a house where the owners were sitting in front of their garage in lawn chairs waiting for the trick-or-treaters to come over. The homeowners were dressed

<96>

in t-shirts and shorts. In the back of my mind, I was thinking, "you're going to mess around and get sick."

"It's a nice day to do this, isn't it?" I said, making small talk while my children grabbed candy.

The homeowners responded: "Yeah, we are from Wisconsin. This is like summer to us."

Their adaptation to the climate was different from mine, and they were just fine. It's the same way with any other situation; once you start thinking over and over again in a direction, you attract everything you need to adapt to that situation so you can be successful or pre-pared for it.

Some people have adapted themselves to under-achieving and don't even know it. They live a life where they are not in proximity to the thing they said they wanted. If you tell them they are underachieving, they won't believe it. It is only in those times of awareness where they step outside of themselves and realize they are not where they want to be, and then they fall further into a depressed state, which often furthers more of the same underachievement.

The universal language of having what you want in life is the emotions you wrap your thoughts in. So if you say you want a new job, that is only words. The only way to turn this set of words into reality is to think only in that direction. Don't think about the hardships you're hav-

<97>

ing, which are causing you to need the job. That is akin to looking back. If a dog was chasing you, would you stop to look back at the dog? You would run non-stop until you reached safety.

Sadly, most people will conjure up a bunch of reasons for why they won't achieve their goals. They focus on the difficulty of reaching their goals, their imperfections, skill deficiencies, and more. All of these thoughts attract their counterparts. Fear of embarrassment attracts instances where people laugh at you or question you with a look of perturbed confusion. Focusing on your skill deficiency attracts self-consciousness and people who are impatient during your learning process. Conversely, confidence attracts instances where people walk up and tell you how well you did. They tell you that they were laughing at the joke you told. They tell you they looked perturbed because what you said really spoke to them and made them want to do better in their own lives.

You see, both thoughts carry the same weight, but they filter experiences differently. After a while, those consistent thoughts become your belief and control your life.

Remember, everyone is abundantly successful, whether they are prospering or failing miserably. They are successfully getting exactly what they think about all day.

<98>

Tip the Scale

Imagine you put two stacks of paper plates on a scale. On the left side, there are five plates, and on the right side, there are 10. To which side do you think the scale would tip? Logically, the side with the most plates should be the heaviest, right?

What if the scale leaned to the side with the five plates instead of the 10 plates, you'd think something was wrong with the scale! Right? Well, what if I told you the plates on the left were made of polished clay while the plates on the right were made of styrofoam? Now would it make sense? Of course, it would.

Those polished clay plates represent thoughts that have been wrapped in emotions. Thoughts alone have little weight. "I want to be successful," "I want to travel." However, when you add emotion to those thoughts, they become heavier. And this works both ways. I can have 10 thoughts of a successful life, but if I have five negative emotions when I think about what it will take for me to achieve that life, the scale will tip towards the negative emotion. I can also have 10 negative thoughts, but if I wrap my five positive thoughts in positive emotions, the scale will tip in my favor.

For example: As I began to build Momentum University, I had grand plans for speaking to companies around the globe. I have dozens of ideas of what a successful business and life looked like for me. However, when I thought about the idea of cold-calling businesses

<99>

and requesting an audience to discuss opportunities, I got nervous. I felt unprepared. I thought about how I hated sales calls and sales in general. My emotions did not line up with what I said I wanted, and as a result, I was not making any connections to expand my business. When you think about what you want to achieve in your life, do you have good emotions about what it will take to achieve those goals, or do you conjure up the negative emotions of fear, embarrassment, uncertainty, and resistance?

Your emotion concerning your life will tip the scale in your favor. The good news is that you can control your emotions. No, you are not helpless to what you feel. I can hear someone now saying, "I can't help how I feel." Yes you can. You can create the emotion you need because your mind really doesn't know the difference. When you allow fear in your mind, your brain pumps out the same hormone (Cortisol)–whether you're afraid to make a phone call or if you're running from a grizzly bear. The brain doesn't care. It's job is to keep you safe and relaxed, so it activates the Flight response.

If you are laughing and enjoying yourself your brain will pump dopamine, a hormone that will induce pleasure, creativity, confidence, and enjoyment. By forcing yourself to find the brighter side to enjoy, to laugh, to pump dopamine, you will create the results you want. Yes, it will take practice. You will feel awkward forcing yourself to celebrate or laugh during challenges, but you

<100>

will eventually learn to tip the scale in your favor.

I can hear some of you now saying how do I turn my life around if it is not going in the direction I want? Great question! Because of such a good question, you deserve a great answer.

Let's do the math.

I understand that some of you may not be thrilled about diving into math, but I promise to keep it light.

-10 -9 -8 -7 -6 -5 -4 -3 -2 -1 **0** 1 2 3 4 5 6 7 8 9 10

Figure 6.1

In Figure 6.1, you'll notice a line with a 0 in the middle. On the left side, there are negative numbers (1-10), and on the right side, an equal amount of positive numbers.

Now, let's envision your life as a numerical plot. If, for instance, you feel like you're a bit behind on things but still hopeful, we'll place you at (-4). If your desired goal in life is at the marked number 10 on the right side, it means you don't just have 10 spaces to cover, but a total of 15 spaces (including the 0).

This leads me to a crucial point: focus on your own journey. When you see someone at +2, they only have 8 positions to advance to reach the same point. If you pay more attention to their progress instead of your own des-

<101>

tination, you might start stacking plates on the opposing side of the scale.

Envy and jealousy can weigh heavily as emotions, and that's not where you want to invest your energy. Save your emotions for the journey you're on. If you're going to invest emotion in others, let it be in the form of support and gratitude for the path they're on. Celebrate their successes.

Now, returning to the analogy of plotting numbers and applying it to your approach to life: if you recognize that you're not where you want to be and feel like you're on the negative side of the plotline, it's crucial to devise a plan tailored to your unique journey to reach your desired destination. Your plotted position will serve as a guide, indicating whether you're close or still some distance away from your goal, and how much effort you need to put in.

Be completely honest with yourself. Ultimately, your life experience hinges on how you perceive it and how you respond to your daily placement in relation to your goal(s).

Thinking causes action:

Everything I've discussed about Momentum may seem theoretical and philosophical unless you put real action behind it. So, let's delve into some of the crucial actions that will keep you winning in the game of life.

Momentum is a tangible force! Consider any sport.

<102>

There are moments in a game where you can unmistakably witness the phenomenon of Momentum in action. You might even hear spectators or announcers say, "this team has the Momentum."

I've witnessed games where one team had a commanding lead until the opposing team made a game-changing play. In that instant, you can identify when the Momentum shifted for the team that was trailing. The sideline atmosphere suddenly fills with hope and excitement. Before you know it, another play is executed, putting the losing team back in contention.

What's intriguing about this juncture in the game is that the leading team is still in the lead, but there's been an emotional shift in the atmosphere signaling them that they're in jeopardy. If they don't halt the Momentum shift, they'll lose their lead. On the flip side, the losing team is still behind, but they're gaining confidence and hope. The players now "believe"... and this, my friends, is when remarkable things can happen.

The same dynamic unfolds in life, but there are no cheering fans to signify a Momentum shift in your favor or against you. You just start noticing unusual occurrences in your life, either remarkably good or regrettably bad. Up until this point, you may have never viewed it in this light.

You might have simply thought to yourself, "hmmm, when it rains, it pours," or "I've been having a streak of bad luck lately." Some might even jest, "I should play the

<103>

lotto today with all this good luck." These are various ways of recognizing the Momentum shifts – whether positive or negative – that are unfolding in a person's life.

Your awareness of these phenomena is crucial. It allows you to either shower your life with gratitude to sustain the Momentum in that direction or endeavor to redirect your energy if you're dissatisfied with the results.

Awareness serves as an immediate gauge of where you stand in life, enabling you to decide what steps to take toward your desired outcome. It's the thinking that follows your awareness that sets apart those who achieve what they desire from those who grow frustrated with life.

Once you grasp that you hold a position of power and influence, life becomes a bit more manageable. It also prompts you to recognize that you can't attribute your outcomes – whether great or not so great – to any- one else. So, if things are going swimmingly in your life, be thankful, but also acknowledge your part in that suc- cess. Similarly, if things are veering in the opposite di- rection, appreciate the chance to learn and acknowledge your duty to steer it towards improvement.

Action follows awareness. So, you get to decide what that action will be. Will you stack plastic plates or place polished clay ones on the scale of life and tip it in your favor? The power is in your hands. What will it be?

<104>

Recipe for Capturing Happiness:

1. Clearly define what you want.
2. Form a vivid mental image of it.
3. Contemplate it regularly.
4. Infuse your thoughts with emotions.
5. Stay conscious of your progress towards your goals.
6. Act in alignment with your objectives.
7. Revel in what you've created.

<105>

CONCLUSION

In this journey we've taken together, we've discovered the incredible strength that comes from being part of a community. We've also learned how important it is to change the way we think about things to make our lives better. The 3X philosophy is really quite simple but really powerful: if you want to do well in life, you need to be willing to both give and receive help.

We've also figured out some practical steps for asking for help in a smart way. We've seen that it's not a sign of weakness, but actually a brave step towards getting better. "Give Before You Get" reminds us that when we help others, we're actually helping ourselves grow too.

As we go through our own journeys, we've come to see how important it is to be ready for success. This means knowing ourselves well and having a clear idea of where we want to go. We've been given some good advice for success, but it's also about making it fit our own unique dreams and goals.

We've discovered that companies hire people for their skills, but those who really make a difference bring something extra – they create value. We've learned how to make an impact and be influential. The "7 Steps to Value Creation" are like a guide that shows us how to make our mark on the world.

<106>

Lastly, we've learned about momentum. It's like pushing a heavy rock – we need to gather the energy and determination to get it moving. With steady effort and a strong commitment, we can build the momentum that takes us closer to our dreams.

Now, as we stand here at this important moment, armed with all we've learned, let's move forward with open hearts. Let's be ready to help and be helped, to create value, and to keep moving towards a future full of purpose, making a real difference. The power is in our hands, and together, we can shape a world full of endless possibilities.

<107>